Pentatonix
CHRISTMAS IS HERE!

ISBN 978-1-5400-4430-3

Visit Hal Leonard Online at
www.halleonard.com

Contact Us:
Hal Leonard
7777 West Bluemound Road
Milwaukee, WI 53213
Email: info@halleonard.com

In Europe contact:
Hal Leonard Europe Limited
42 Wigmore Street
Marylebone, London, W1U 2RN
Email: info@halleonardeurope.com

In Australia contact:
Hal Leonard Australia Pty. Ltd.
4 Lentara Court
Cheltenham, Victoria, 3192 Australia
Email: info@halleonard.com.au

WHAT CHRISTMAS MEANS TO ME

Words and Music by GEORGE GORDY,
ALLEN STORY and ANNA GORDY GAYE

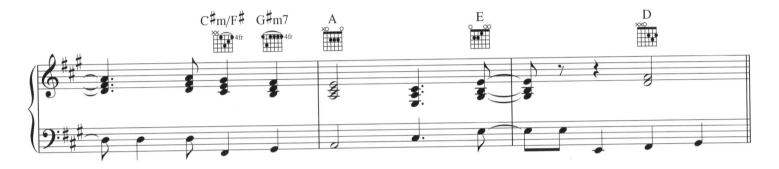

Can - dles burn - in' low, _____ lots of mis - tle - toe. _____

Lots of snow _____ and ice _____

ev - 'ry - where __ we go. __ (Ev - 'ry - where you go.) Choirs __ sing - in' car -

- ols right out - side __ my door. __ (Right out - side my

All these things and more, _____ all these things and more, __
door.)

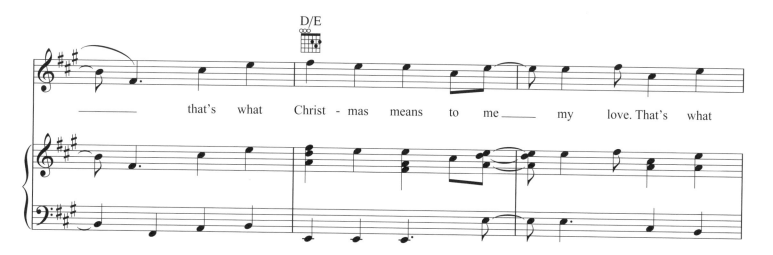

_____ that's what Christ - mas means to me ___ my love. That's what

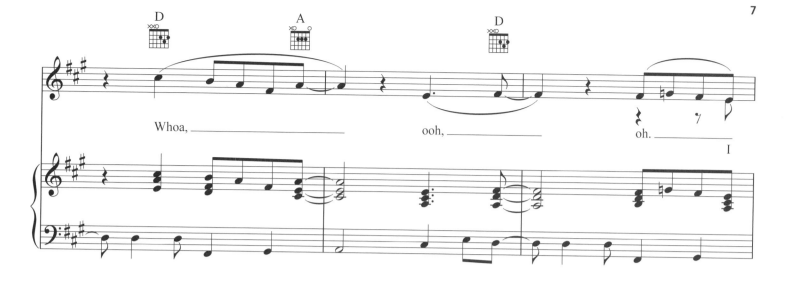

Whoa, _____ ooh, _____ oh. _____ I

see your smil - in' face ____ like I've nev - er ____ seen ____ be - fore. ____

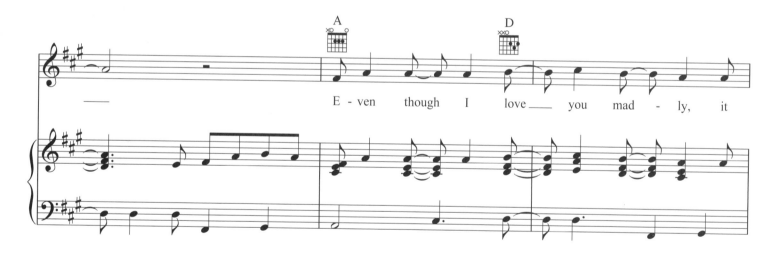

____ E - ven though I love ____ you mad - ly, it

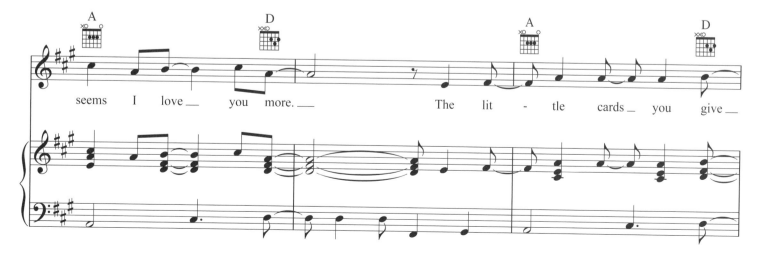

seems I love ____ you more. ____ The lit - tle cards ____ you give ____

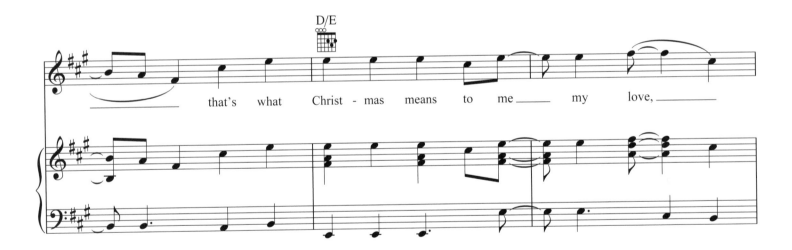

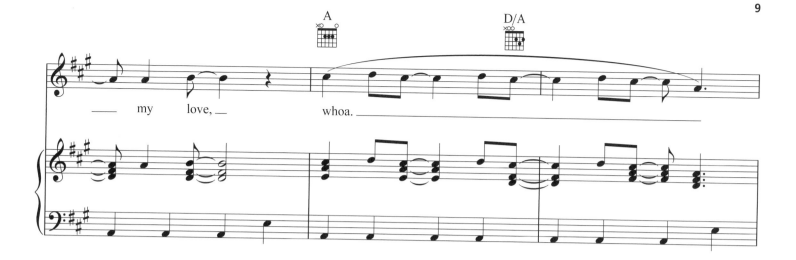

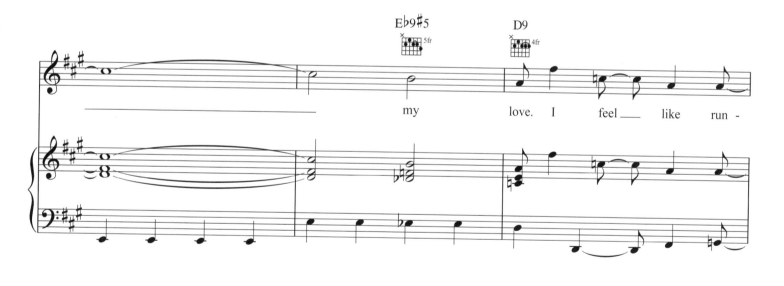

Deck the halls __ with hol - ly, sing - in' Sil - ent Night. __

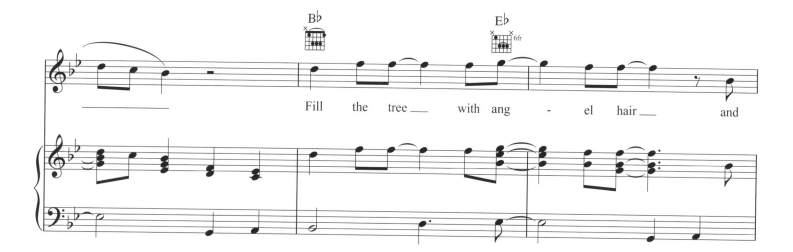

__ Fill the tree __ with ang - el hair __ and

pret - ty, pret - ty lights. _____ Go to sleep __ and wake __

__ up just be - fore __ day - light. __

All these things and more, _____ all these things and more __

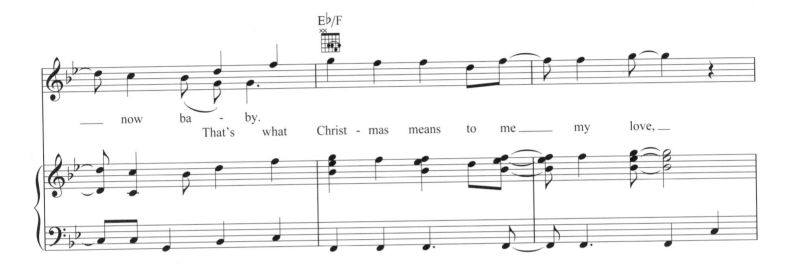

__ now ba - by. That's what Christ - mas means to me ___ my love, __

Christ - mas means to me ___ my love. __ Christ - mas means to me ___ my love, _

oh. _____ Christ - mas means to me ___ my love, _

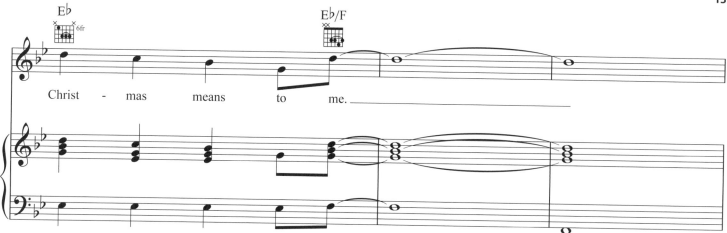

Christ - mas means to me.

Christ - mas means to me _____ my love, _____ oh. _____

Christ - mas means to me _____ my love, _____

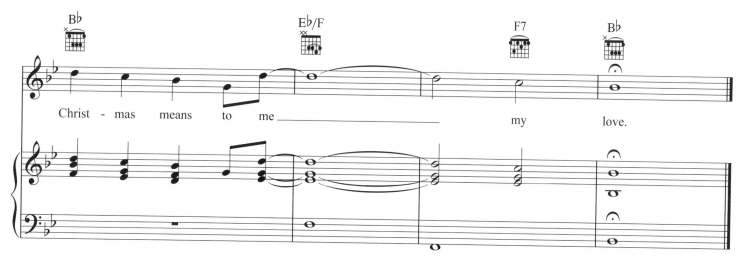

Christ - mas means to me _____ my love.

ROCKIN' AROUND
THE CHRISTMAS TREE

Music and Lyrics by
JOHNNY MARKS

Moderate groove

Oh, __ we're rock-in' a-round __ the

Christ-mas tree __ at the Christ-mas par-ty hop. __

mis - tle - toe hung where you can see, ev - 'ry cou - ple tries to stop.

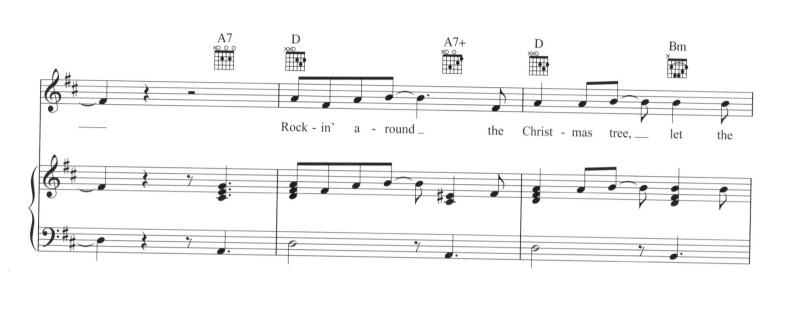

Rock - in' a - round the Christ - mas tree, let the

Christ - mas spir - it ring. Lat - er we'll have some

pump - kin pie and we'll do some car - ol - ing. Oh,

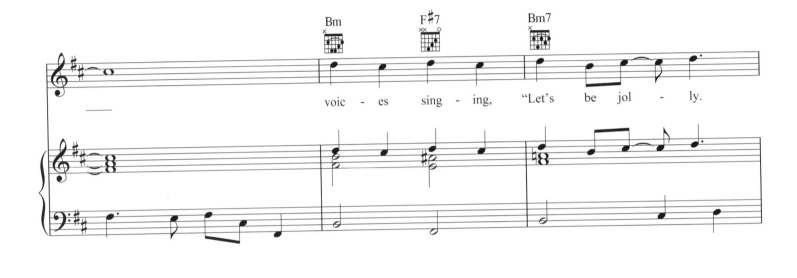

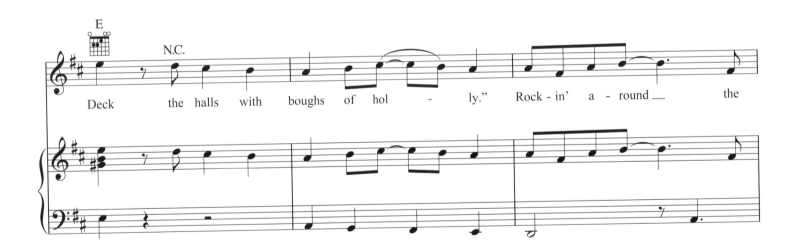

Ev - 'ry-one's danc - ing merr - i - ly ___ in the new old fash - ioned way. __

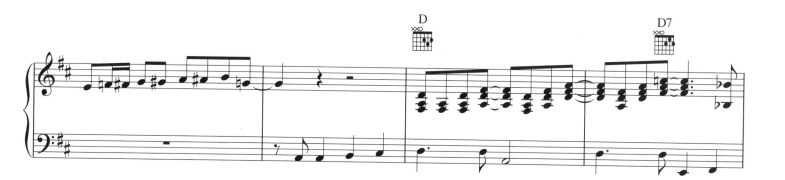

boughs of hol - ly." Rock - in' a - round ___ the Christ - mas tree, ___ have a

hap - py hol - i - day. ___ Ev - 'ry - one's danc - in'

merr - i - ly ___ in the new old fash - ioned ___ way. ___

yeah. ___

IT'S BEGINNING TO LOOK
A LOT LIKE CHRISTMAS

By MEREDITH WILLSON

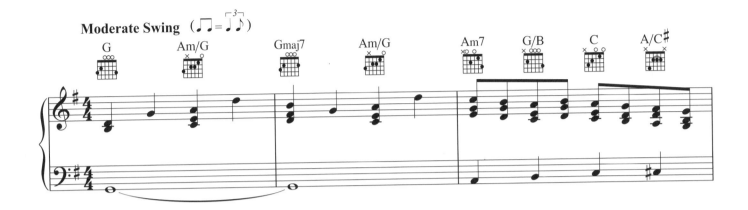

It's be - gin-ning to look a lot like Christ - mas

ev - 'ry-where you go.   Take a   look at the Five and Ten

glis-ten-ing once a - gain with can-dy canes and sil - ver lanes a - glow. It's be -

gin - ning to look a lot like Christ - mas, toys in ev - 'ry

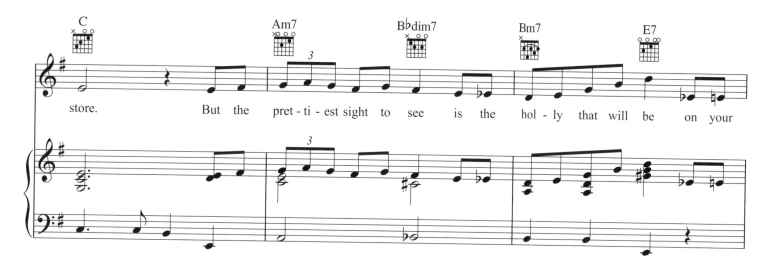

store. But the pret - ti - est sight to see is the hol - ly that will be on your

own front door. A pair of hop-a-long boots and a pis-tol that shoots is the

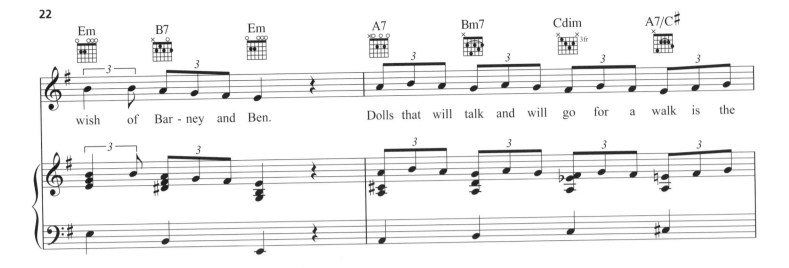

wish of Bar - ney and Ben. Dolls that will talk and will go for a walk is the

hope of Jan-ice and Jen. And Mom and Dad can hard-ly wait for school to start a - gain. It's be -

gin - ning to look a lot like Christ - mas ev - 'ry-where you

go. There's a tree in the Grand Ho - tel, one in the park as well. The

stur - dy kind that does-n't mind the snow. It's be - ginn-ing to look a lot like

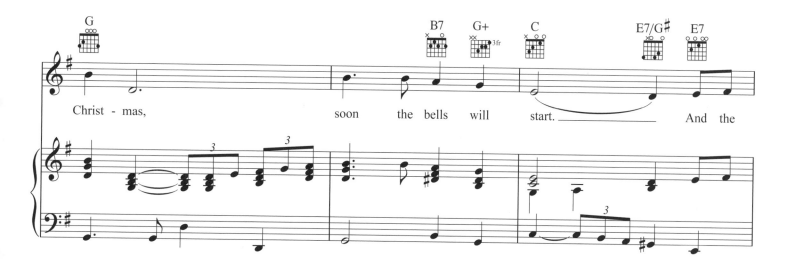

Christ - mas, soon the bells will start. _____ And the

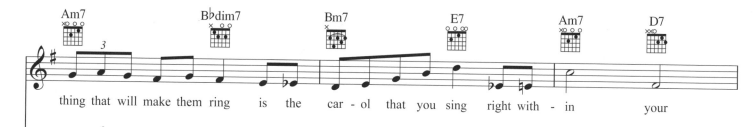

thing that will make them ring is the car - ol that you sing right with - in your

heart.

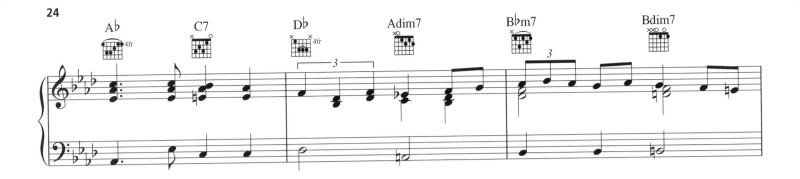

A pair of

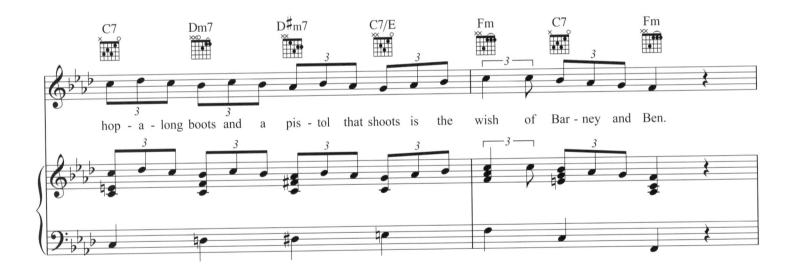

hop - a - long boots and a pis - tol that shoots is the wish of Bar - ney and Ben.

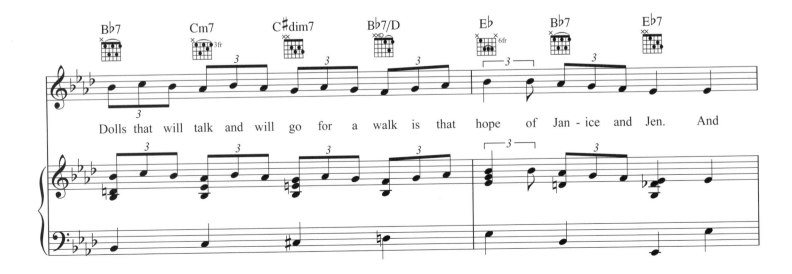

Dolls that will talk and will go for a walk is that hope of Jan - ice and Jen. And

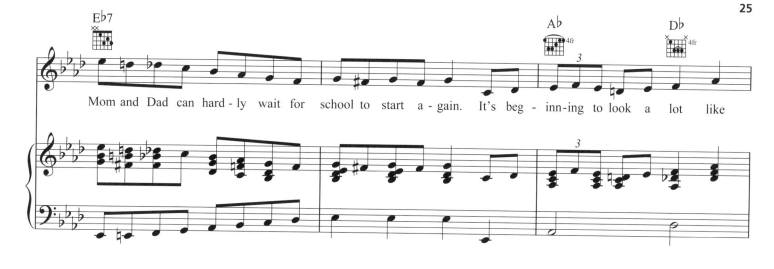

Mom and Dad can hard-ly wait for school to start a-gain. It's beg-inn-ing to look a lot like

Christ-mas, _____ soon the bells will start. And the thing that will make them ring is the

car-ol that you sing right with-in your heart. _____

Oh yeah. _

GROWN-UP CHRISTMAS LIST

Words and Music by DAVID FOSTER
and LINDA THOMPSON-JENNER

Moderately fast

Do do do do do, do do do do do do do do do do do

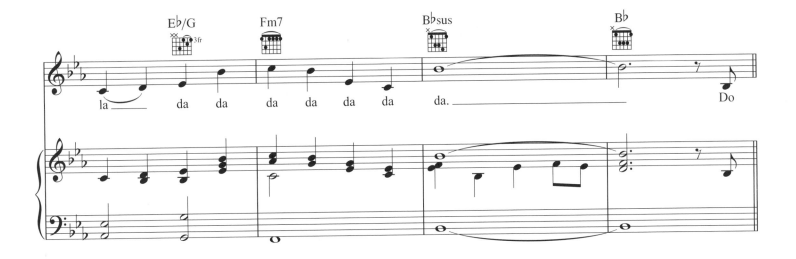

la da da da da da da da. Do

you re-mem-ber me? I sat up-on your knee? I

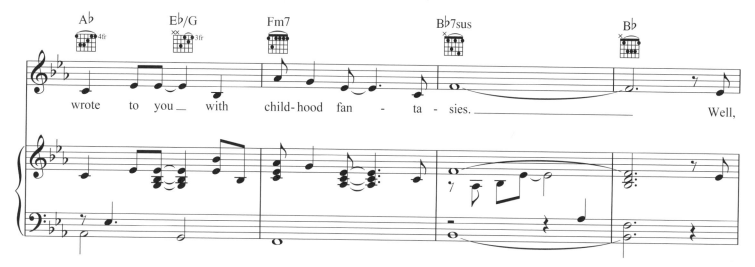

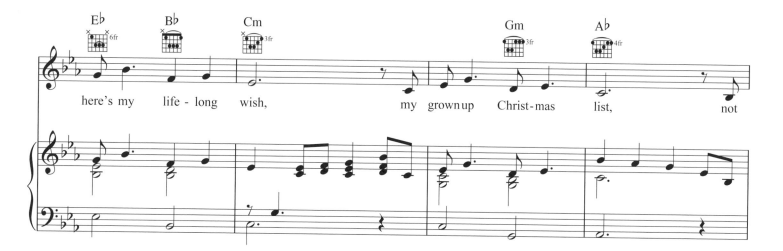

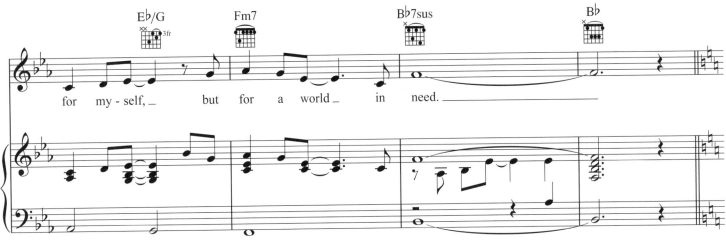

for my-self, __ but for a world __ in need. _____

No more lives __ torn __ a-part, _____ that wars __ would nev - er start __

__ and time would heal __ all hearts _____

And ev - 'ry - one would have __ a friend _____ and

right would al - ways win _____ and love would nev - er end,

To Coda

this is my grown - up Christ - mas list. _____

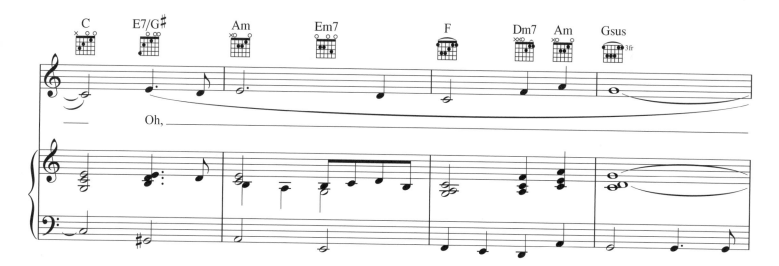

Oh, _____

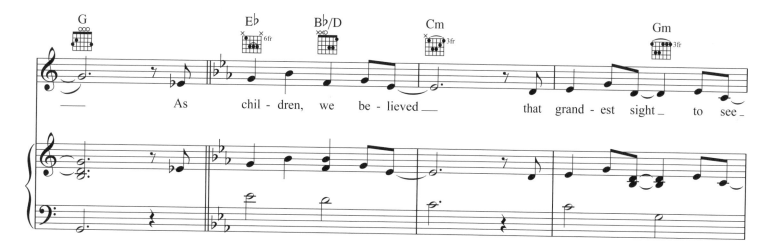

As chil - dren, we be - lieved _____ that grand - est sight __ to see __

was some-thing love-ly wrapped be-neath our tree.

But heav-en on-ly knows that

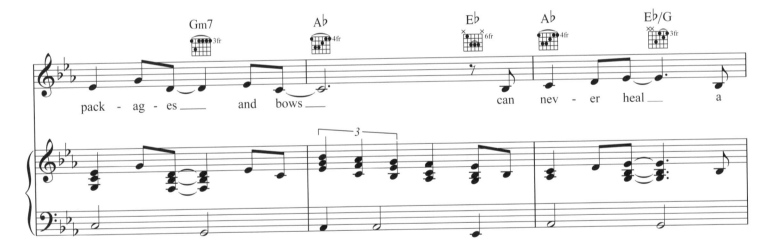

pack-ag-es and bows can nev-er heal a

hurt-ing hu-man soul.

D.S. al Coda

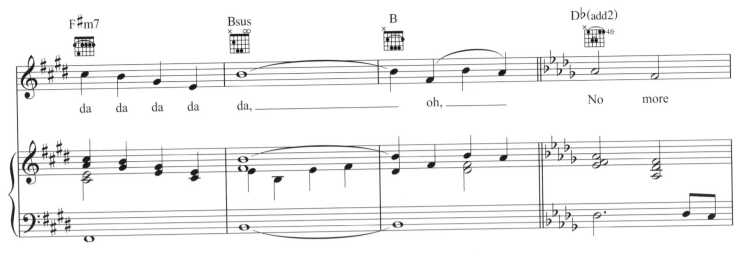

da da da da da, _____ oh, _____ No more

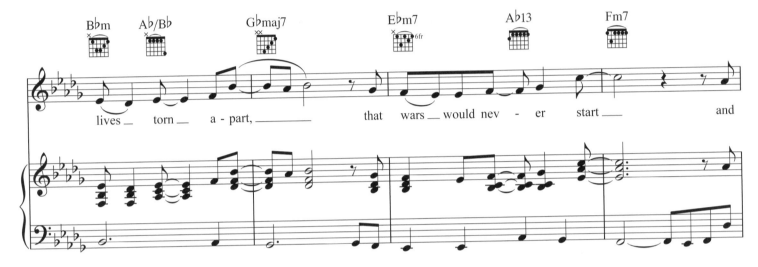

lives __ torn __ a - part, _____ that wars __ would nev - er start __ and

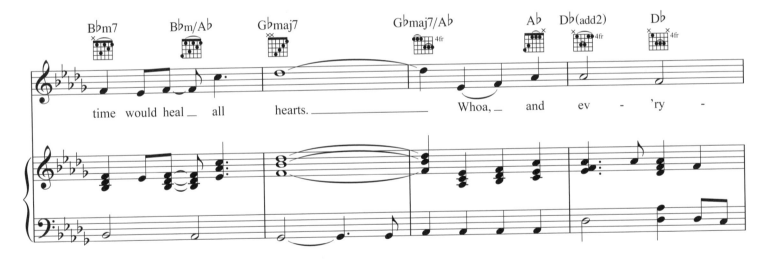

time would heal __ all hearts. _____ Whoa, __ and ev - 'ry -

one would have __ a friend _____ and right would al - ways win __

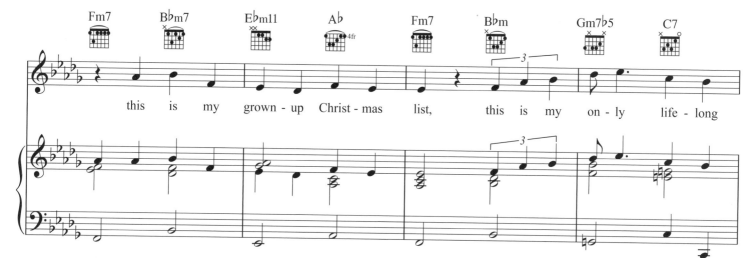

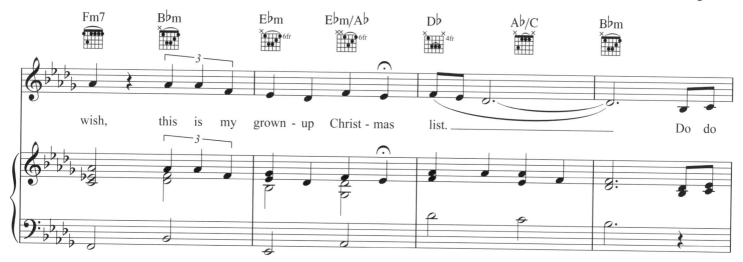

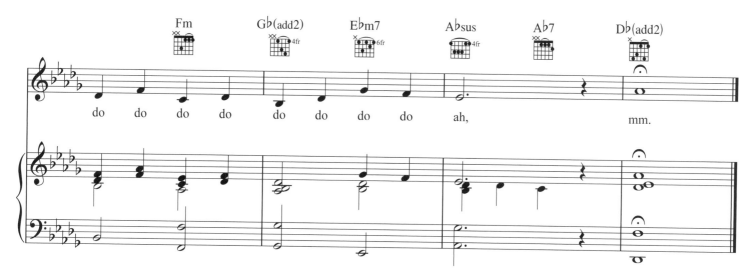

GREENSLEEVES

TRADITIONAL
Arranged by PTX
and BEN BRAM

Moderate Waltz, with feeling

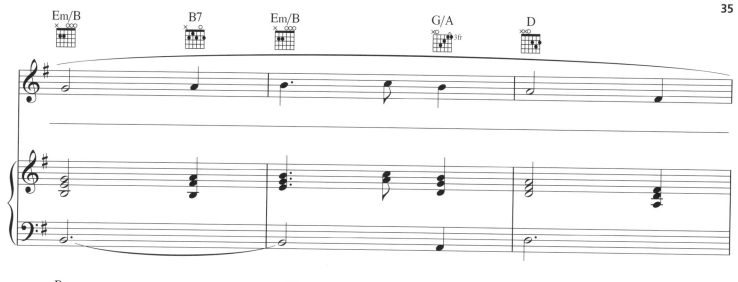

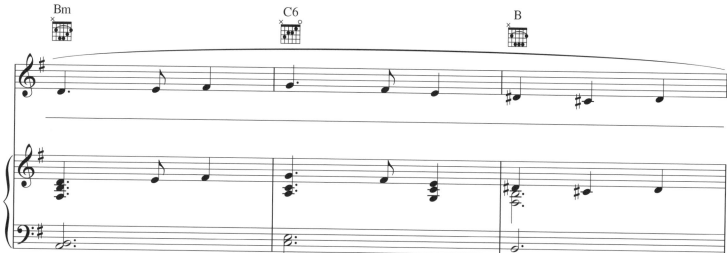

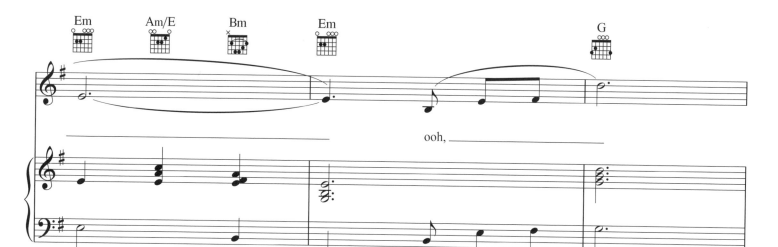

ooh,

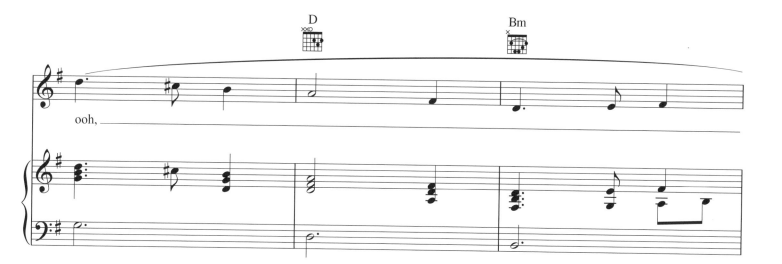

ooh,

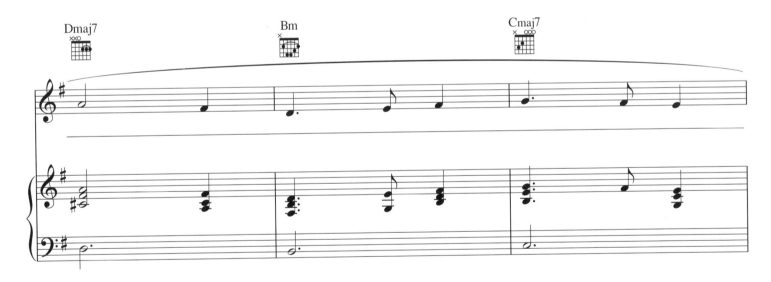

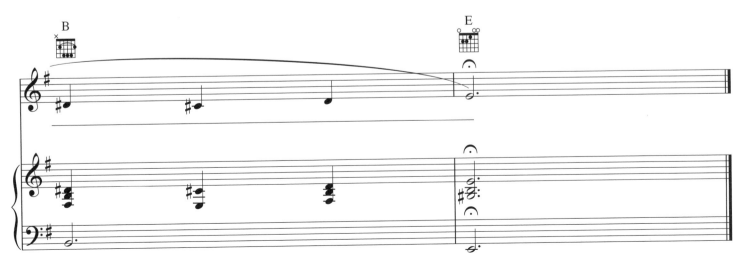

WHEN YOU BELIEVE

from THE PRINCE OF EGYPT

Words and Music by
STEPHEN SCHWARTZ

Moderately fast

Man-y nights we've prayed with

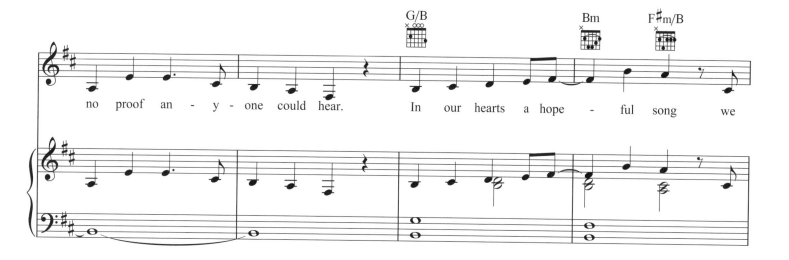

no proof an-y-one could hear. In our hearts a hope-ful song we

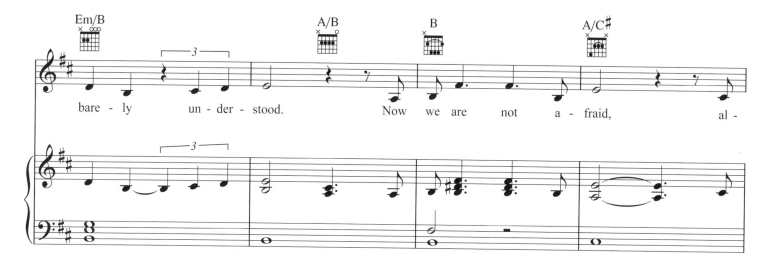

bare-ly un-der-stood. Now we are not a-fraid, al-

though we know there's much to fear.__ We were mov-ing moun-tains long be-

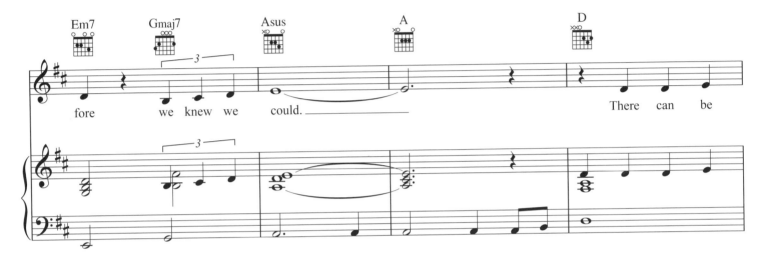

fore we knew we could._____ There can be

mir - a - cles when you be - lieve. Though __ hope is

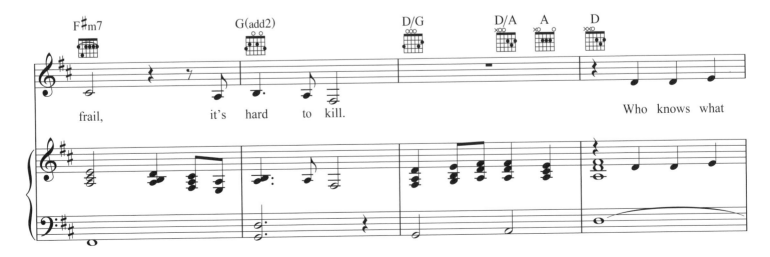

frail, it's hard to kill. Who knows what

mir - a - cles __ you can a - chieve. When you __ be -

lieve, some - how you will. _____ You will when

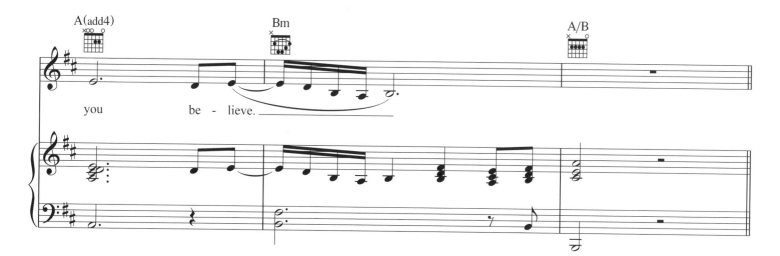

you be - lieve. _____

In this time of fear when prayer so of - ten proved __ in vain, __

There can be mir - a - cles when you be - lieve.

Though __ hope is frail, it's hard to kill.

Who knows what mir - a - cles __

you __ can a - chieve. __ When you be - lieve, __

some - how you will, _____

you _____ will _____ when _____ you _____ be - lieve.

They don't al - ways hap - pen when _____ you _____ ask. _____

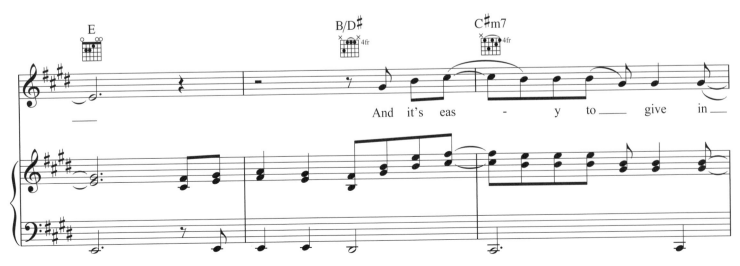

And it's eas - y to _____ give in _____

to your fears. _____ But when _

_____ you're blind - ed by _____ the pain, _ can't see _____ your way _ clear through

the rain, _____ a small _ but still re - sil - ient voice says

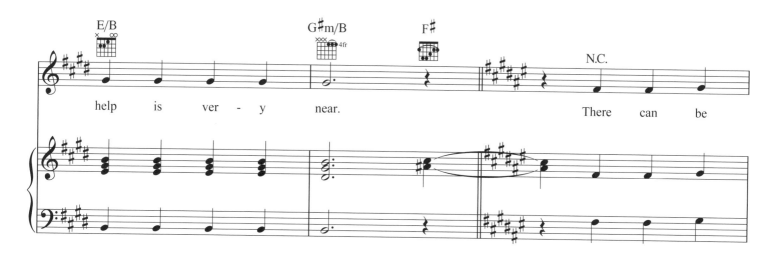

help is ver - y near. There can be

mir - a - cles   when you be - lieve. (When you ___ be -

lieve.) Though hope is frail,   it's hard to kill. It's

hard ___ to kill. ___   Who knows what mir - a - cles ___

you can a - chieve.   When you be -

lieve,   some - how   you   will.   Whoa, _____

now   you   will.   Whoa, _____   you   will   when

you _____   be - lieve. _____

You   will   when   you _____   be - lieve. _____

SWEATER WEATHER

Words and Music by JESSE RUTHERFORD,
ZACHARY ABELS and JEREMY FREEDMAN

All I am is a man. I want the world in my hands.

I hate the beach, but I stand in Cal-i-for-

nia with my toes in the sand. Use the sleeve of my sweat-er. Let's have an ad-ven-

-ture. Head in the clouds, __ but my grav-i-ty's cen - tered. __ Touch my __

neck and I'll touch yours. __ You in those lit - tle high __ waist - ed __

B7   D/C   C

shorts. __ She knows why I think a - bout. __

Am   Em

And what I think a - bout, __ one love, __ two mouths,

one love, — one house, no shirt, no blouse, just us, you find out —

noth-in' that I would-n't wan-na tell you a-bout, — no. _____ 'Cause it's too

cold _____ for you here. And

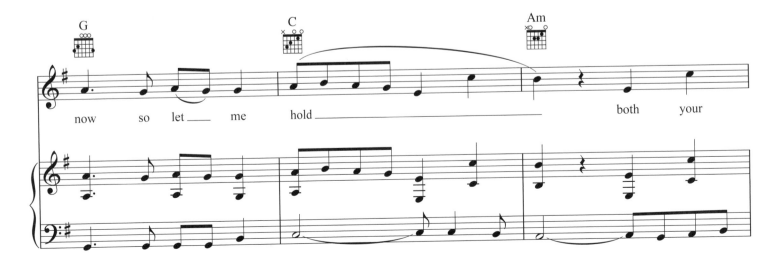

now so let __ me hold _____ both your

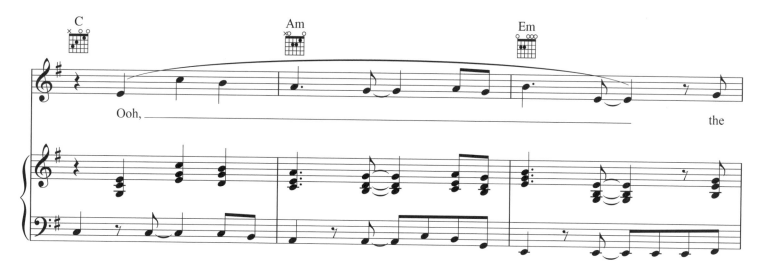

I don't mind if there's not much to say. ___ Some - times the si - lence guides a mind ___ to

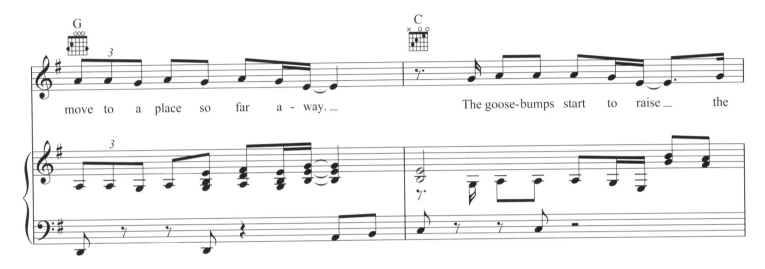

move to a place so far a - way. ___ The goose-bumps start to raise ___ the

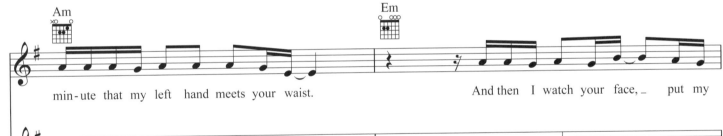

min - ute that my left hand meets your waist. And then I watch your face, ___ put my

fin - ger on your tongue 'cause you love the taste, ___ yeah. ___ These hearts a - dore ___

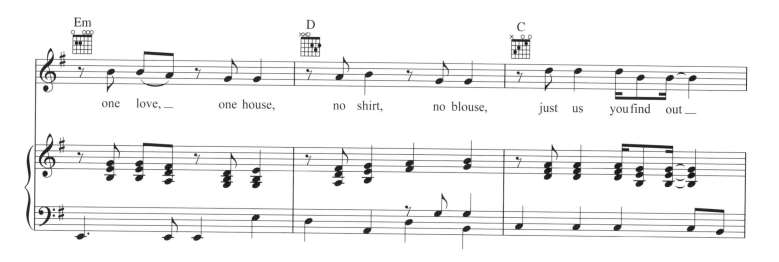

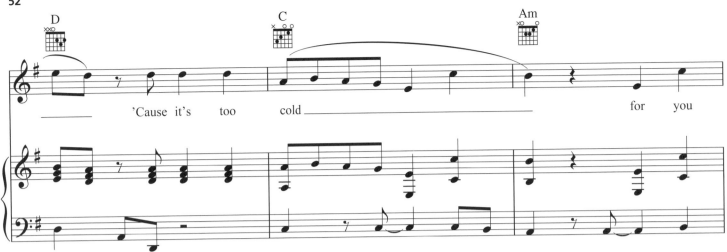

'Cause it's too cold _____ for you

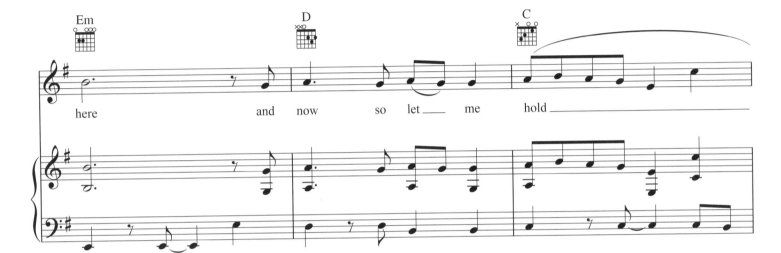

here _____ and now so let ___ me hold _____

_____ both your hands ___ in ___ the holes of my sweat - er. Too

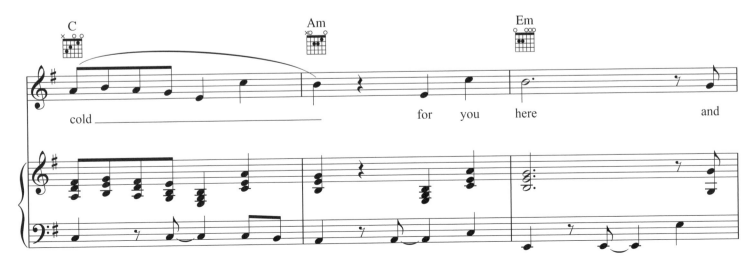

cold _____ for you here _____ and

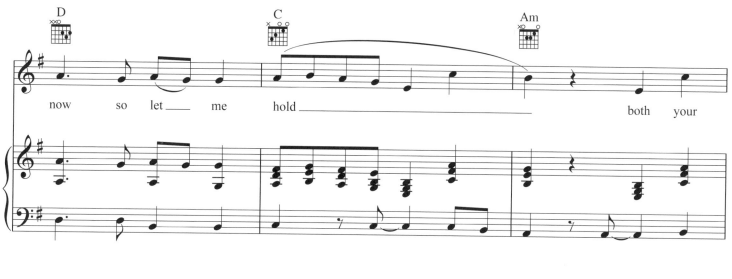

now so let ___ me hold _____ both your

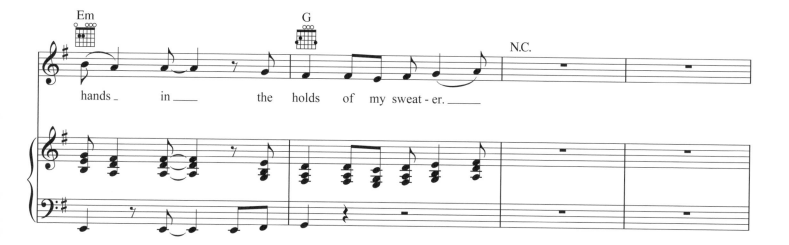

hands ___ in ___ the holds of my sweat - er. _____

Ooh, _____ the

holes of my sweat - er. She knows what I think a - bout ___

and what I think a - bout, __ one love, __ two mouths,

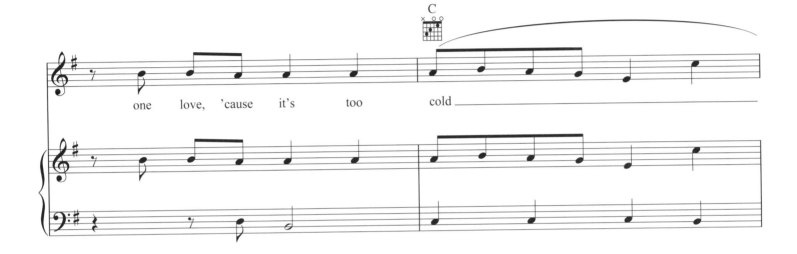

one love, 'cause it's too cold __ for you here

and now so let __ me

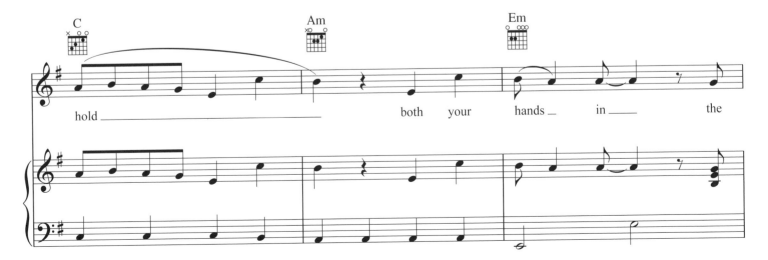

hold __ both your hands __ in __ the

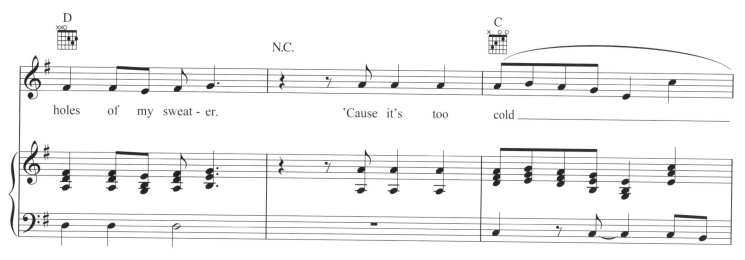

holes of my sweat-er. 'Cause it's too cold _____

_____ for you here and now so let ___ me

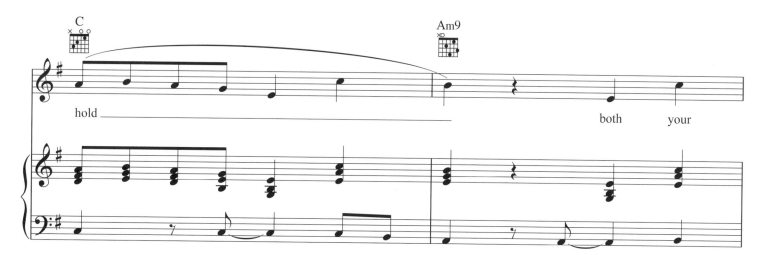

hold _____ both your

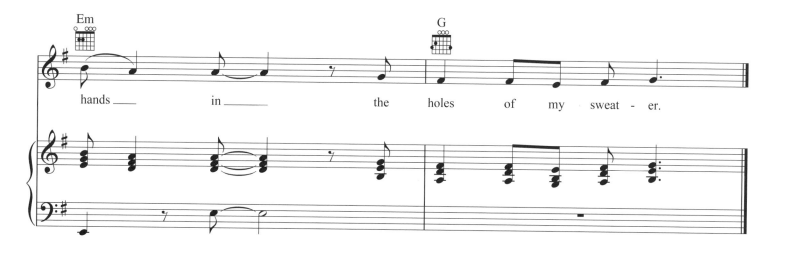

hands ___ in _____ the holes of my sweat - er.

WALTZ OF THE FLOWERS

By PYOTR IL'YICH TCHAIKOVSKY
Arranged by PTX and BEN BRAM

duh ba duh ba duh ba duh ba duh ba duh ba duh ba, duh ba duh ba duh ba.

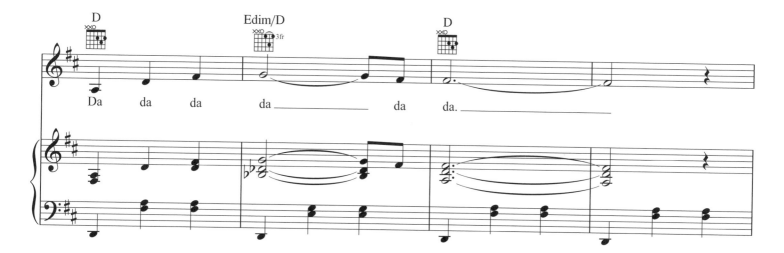

Da da da da _____ da da. _____

Da da da da da da da da. Duh ba dub ba

duh ba duh ba duh, duh ba duh ba duh ba duh ba duh, duh ba duh ba

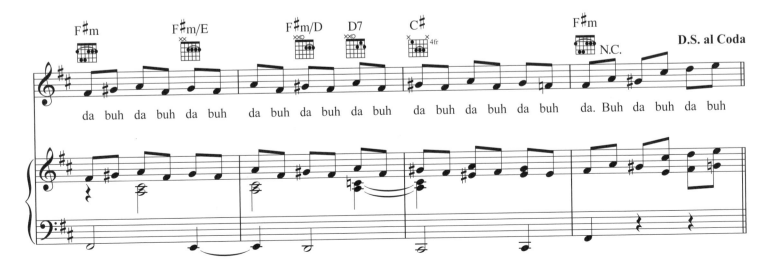

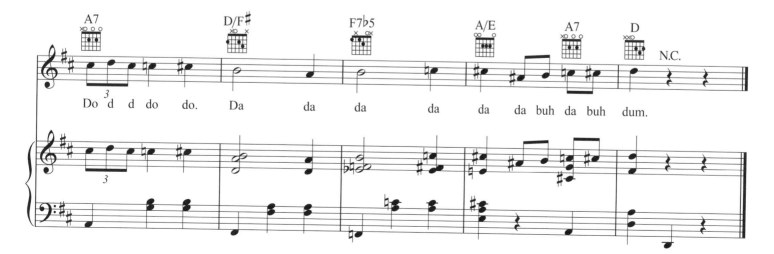

HERE COMES SANTA CLAUS
(Right Down Santa Claus Lane)

Words and Music by GENE AUTRY
and OAKLEY HALDEMAN

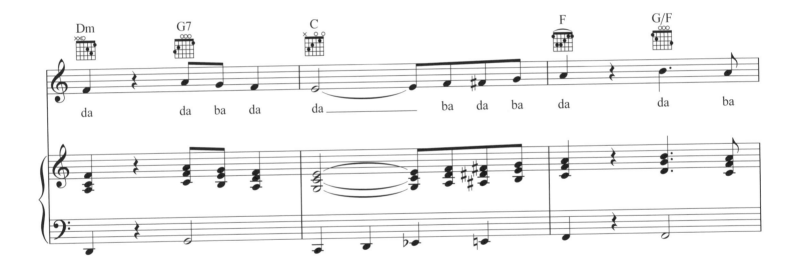

* Recorded a half step higher.

Here comes San - ta Claus, here comes San - ta Claus

right down San - ta Claus Lane. Vix - en and Blit - zen and

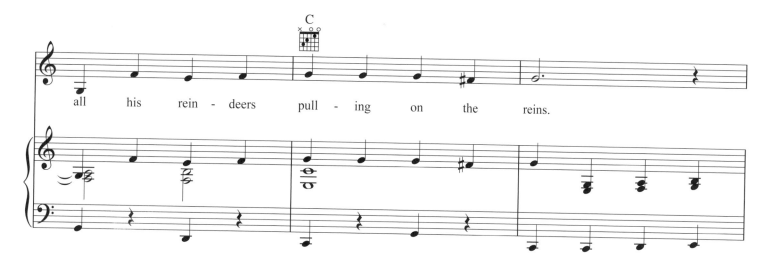

all his rein - deers pull - ing on the reins.

Bells are ring - ing, chil - dren sing - ing, all is mer - ry and

bright. So hang your stock - ings and say your prayers 'cause

San - ta Claus comes to - night. ___ Mer - ry

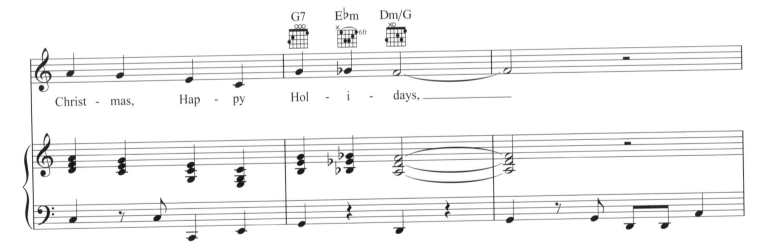

Christ - mas, Hap - py Hol - i - days, ___

Mer - ry Christ - mas, Hap - py Hol - i - days. ___

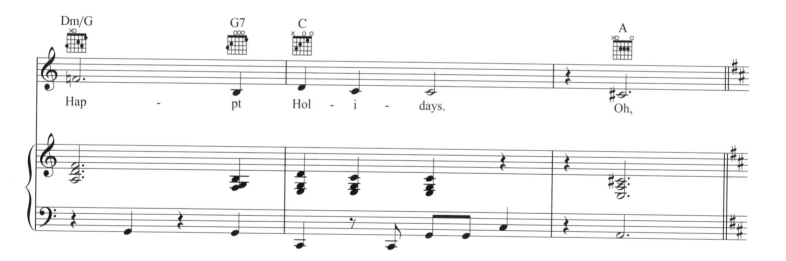

Lane. He's got a bag that's filled with toys for

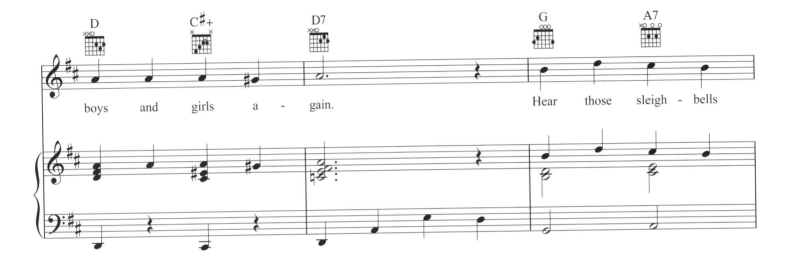

boys and girls a - gain. Hear those sleigh - bells

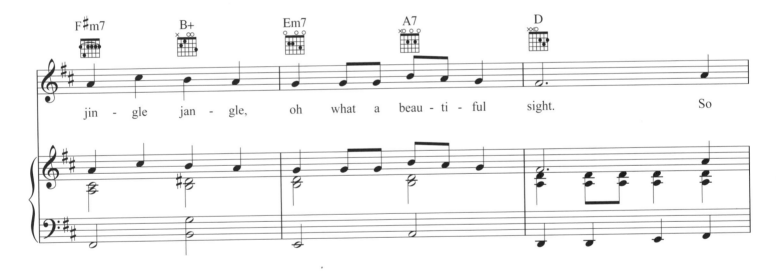

jin - gle jan - gle, oh what a beau - ti - ful sight. So

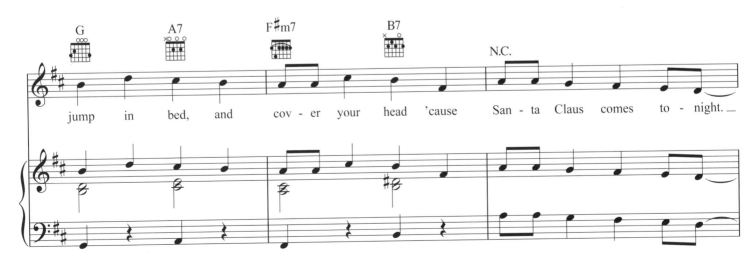

jump in bed, and cov - er your head 'cause San - ta Claus comes to - night.

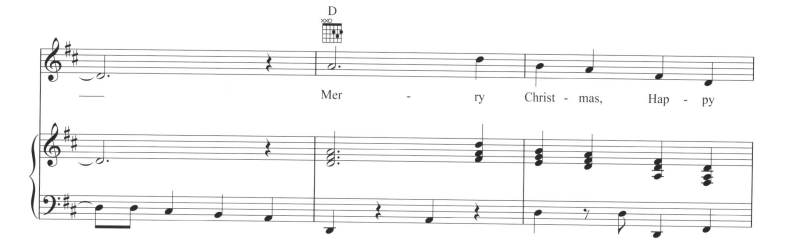

Mer - ry Christ - mas, Hap - py

Hol - i - days, (Ba da da do dee do) Mer - ry

Christ - mas, Hap - py Hol - i - days. (Ba do dn do dee do)

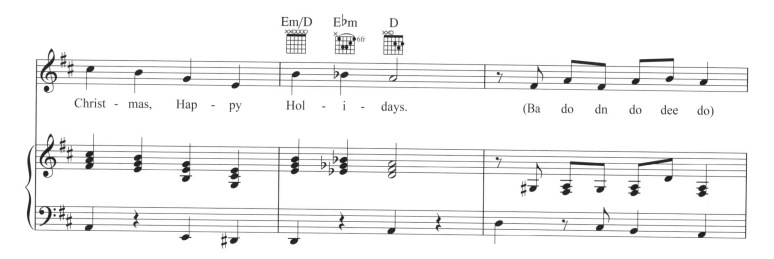

Mer - ry Christ - mas, Hap - py Hol - i - days, _____

Mer - ry Christ - mas, Hap - py

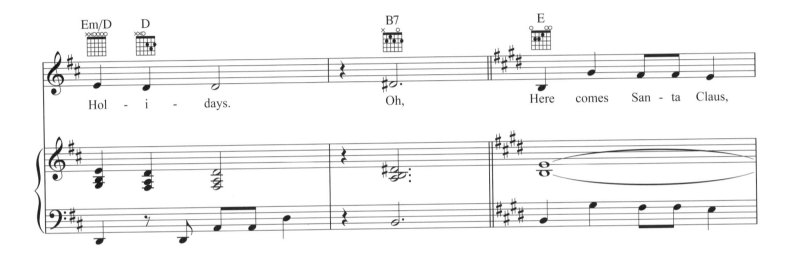

Hol - i - days. Oh, Here comes San - ta Claus,

here comes San - ta Claus, right down San - ta Claus Lane.

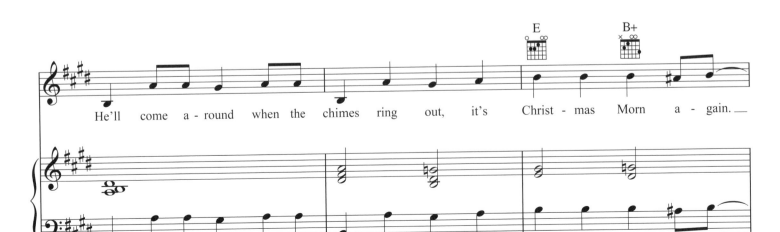

He'll come a - round when the chimes ring out, it's Christ - mas Morn a - gain.

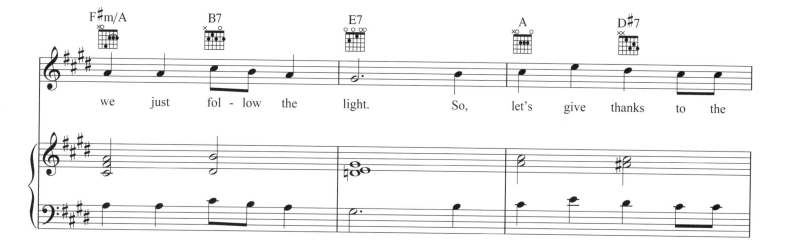

Much slower

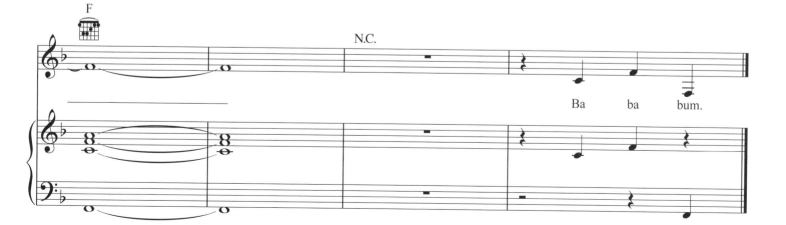

MAKING CHRISTMAS

from THE NIGHTMARE BEFORE CHRISTMAS

Music and Lyrics by
DANNY ELFMAN

Mak - ing Christ - mas, mak - ing Christ - mas.

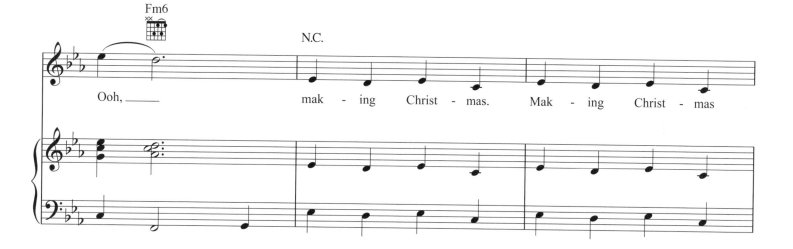

Ooh, _____ mak - ing Christ - mas. Mak - ing Christ - mas

is so fine. It's ours this time and won't the chil - dren

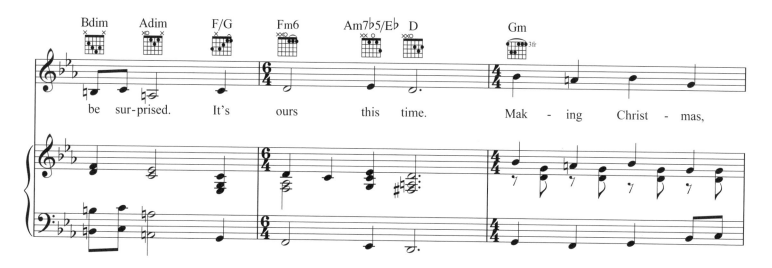

be sur - prised. It's ours this time. Mak - ing Christ - mas,

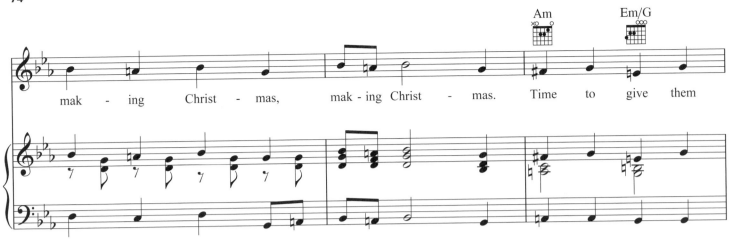

mak - ing Christ - mas, mak - ing Christ - mas. Time to give them

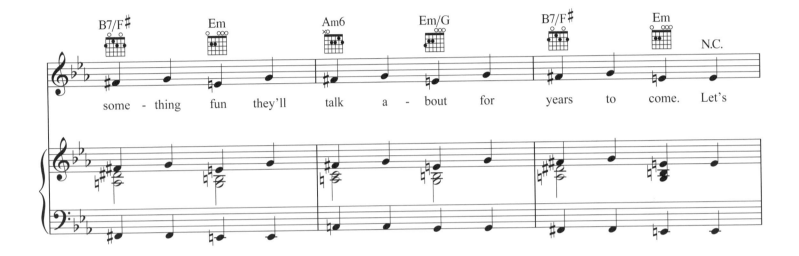

some - thing fun they'll talk a - bout for years to come. Let's

have a cheer from ev - 'ry - one.

Snakes and mice get wrapped up so nice _____ with spi - der

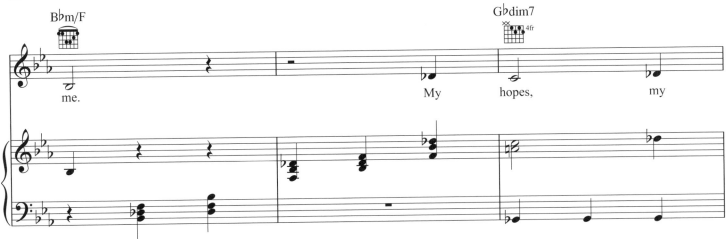

to a most de - light - ful hat. My

com - pli - ments from me to you on this your most in - trigu - ing hat. __ Con -

sid - er though this sub - sti - tute, a bat in place of this old rat. __ *Huh! No, no, no.* Now,

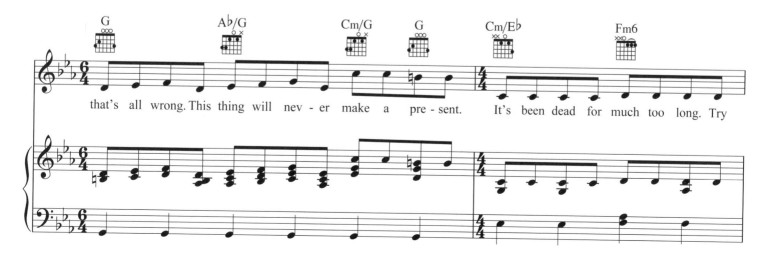

that's all wrong. This thing will nev - er make a pre - sent. It's been dead for much too long. Try

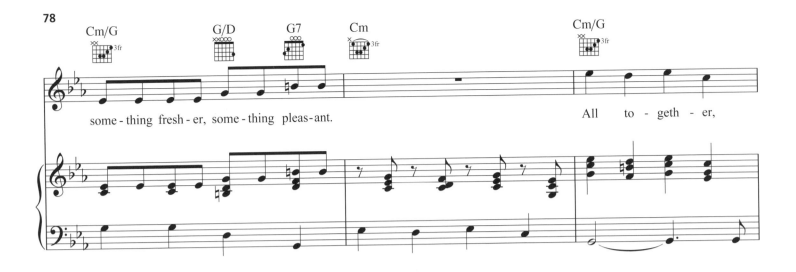

JINGLE BELLS

Words and Music by JAMES S. PIERPONT
Arranged by JACK GOLD and MARTY PAICH
Adapted by PTX and BEN BRAM

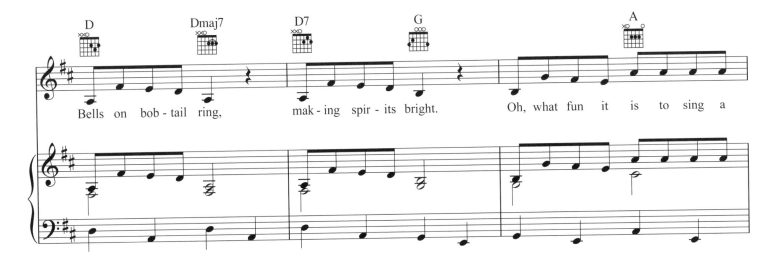

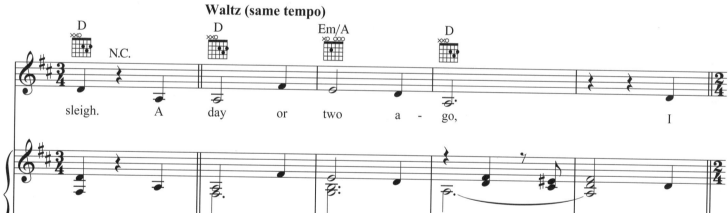

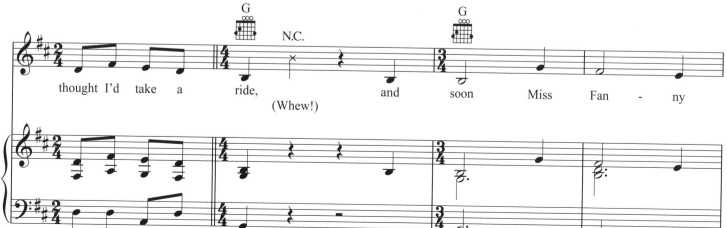

Bright was seat-ed by my side. (Whew!) The

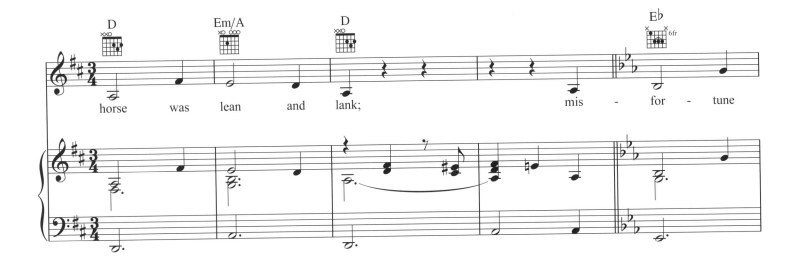

horse was lean and lank; mis - for - tune

seemed his lot. He got in - to a

drift - ing bank and then we got up -

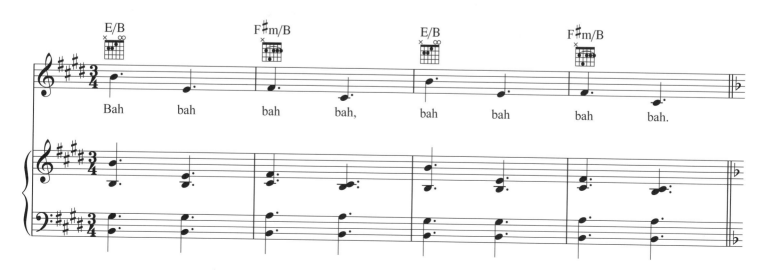

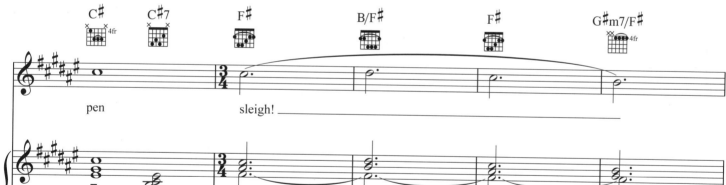

WHERE ARE YOU CHRISTMAS?

from DR. SEUSS' HOW THE GRINCH STOLE CHRISTMAS

Words and Music by WILL JENNINGS,
JAMES HORNER and MARIAH CAREY

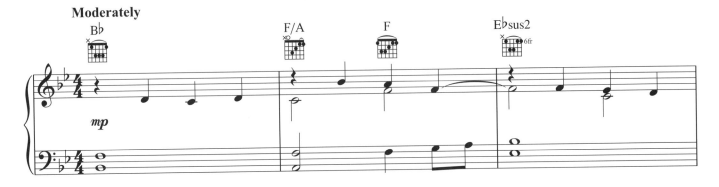

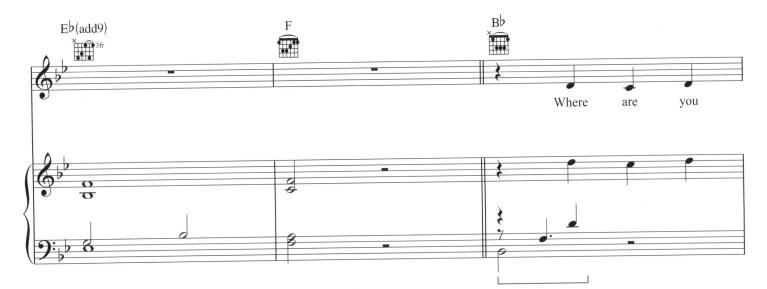

Where are you

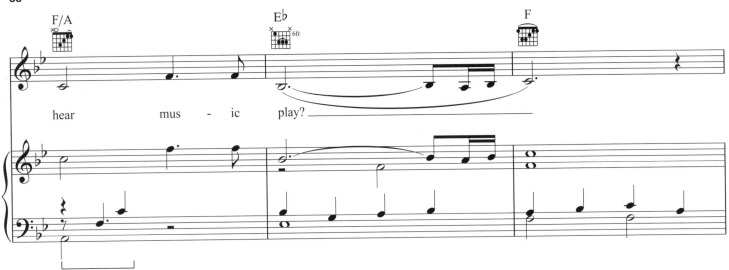

hear mus - ic play? _____

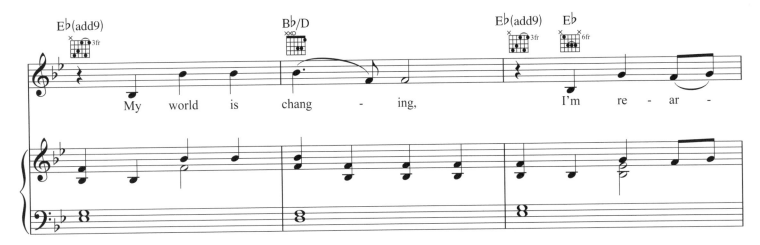

My world is chang - ing, I'm re - ar -

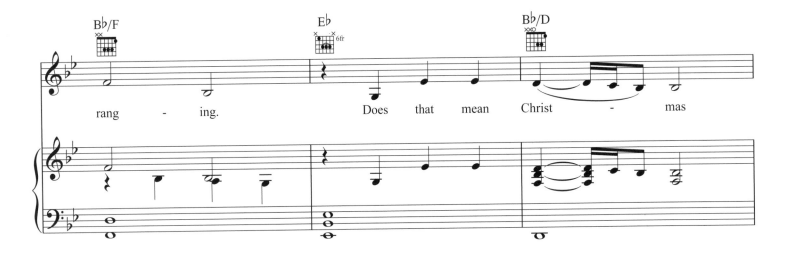

rang - ing. Does that mean Christ - mas

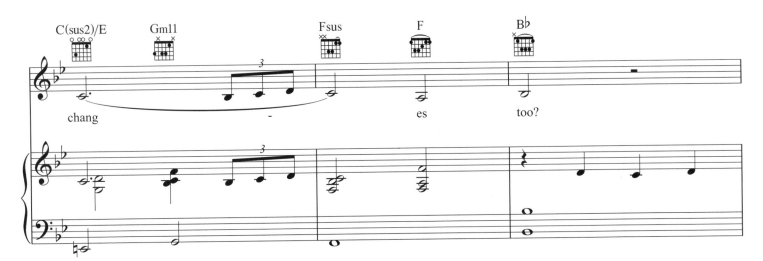

chang - es too?

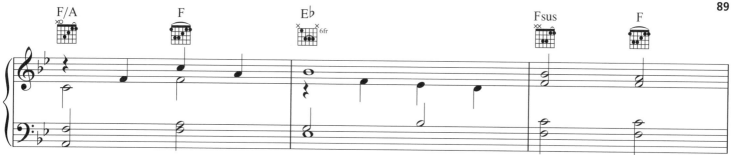

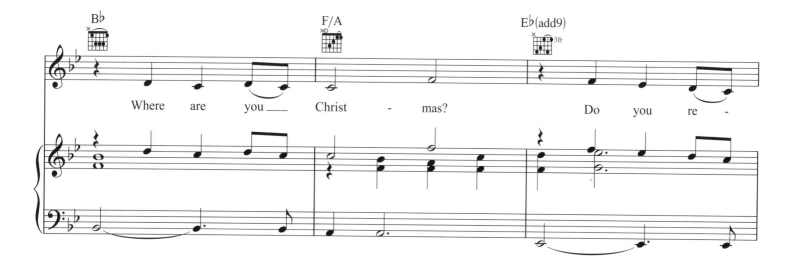

Where are you ___ Christ - mas? Do you re -

mem - ber ___ the one you ___ used to

know? _____ I'm not the

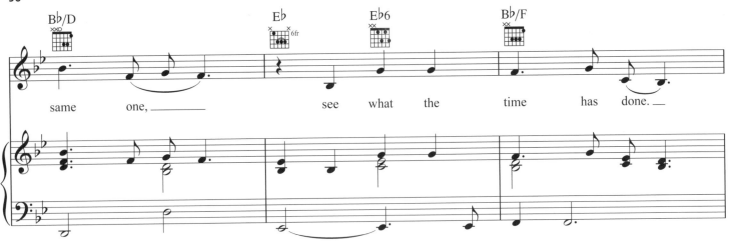

same one, _____ see what the time has done. ___

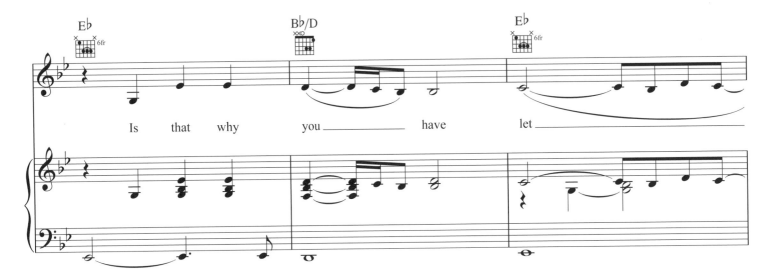

Is that why you _____ have let _____

me go? Oh, _____

Christ - mas is here _____ ev - 'ry - where. _____ Oh, _____

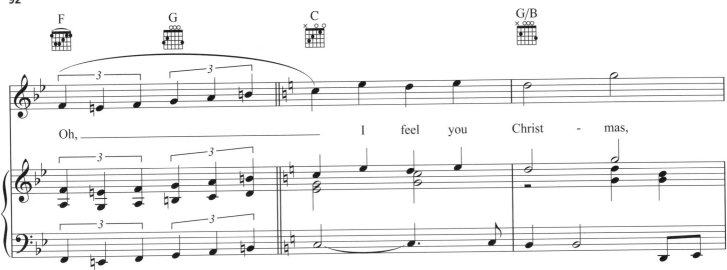

Oh, _____ I feel you Christ - mas,

I know I found _____ you. You nev - er

fade a - way. _____

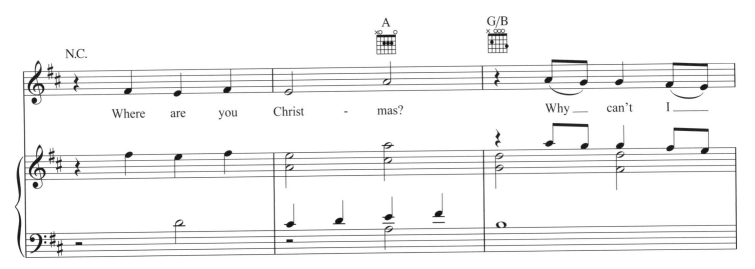

Where are you Christ - mas? Why ___ can't I _____

find _____ you?   Why   have   you _____ gone   a -

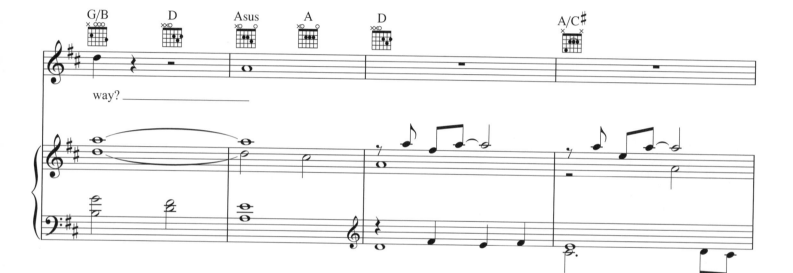

way? _____

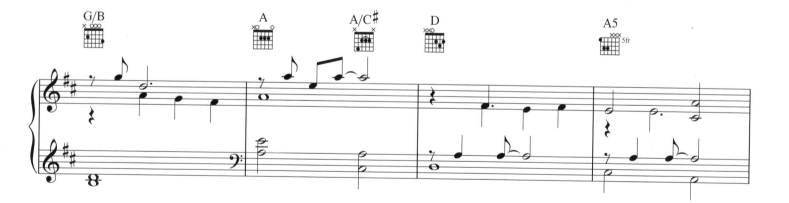

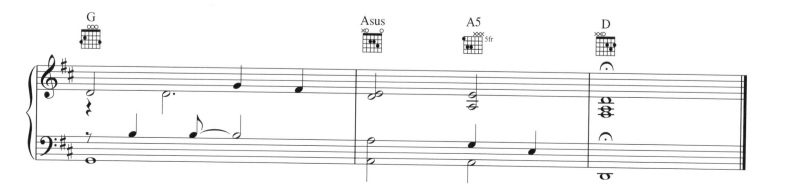

MORE GREAT SONGBOOKS FROM PENTATONIX

PENTATONIX – PTX

Winners of the third season of NBC's *The Sing-Off*, this third album from Texas-based a cappella group Pentatonix is presented here in arrangements with chord symbols, lead vocal lines and the full vocal harmonies transcribed into the piano part. Songs include: Hey Momma/Hit the Road Jack • I Need Your Love • Love Again • Natural Disaster • Run to You • Valentine • and more.

00124862 P/V/G..$17.99

A PENTATONIX CHRISTMAS

This 2016 holiday release by a cappella pop sensation Pentatonix reached #1 on the Billboard® 200 album charts and includes two new original songs, "Good to Be Bad" and "The Christmas Sing-Along." Our collection includes both of these songs plus 9 more in arrangements for piano, voice and guitar: Coldest Winter • Coventry Carol • God Rest Ye Merry Gentlemen • Hallelujah • I'll Be Home for Christmas • Merry Christmas, Happy Holidays • O Come, All Ye Faithful • Up on the Housetop • White Christmas.

00236226 P/V/G..$17.99

PENTATONIX – VOL. III

Six songs from the 2014 album by these 2011 winners of the NBC show *The Sing-Off*. These complete keyboard arrangements feature chord symbols, lead vocal lines, and full vocal harmonies from the following selections from this release which peaked at #5 on the Billboard® 200 Album Charts: La La Latch • On My Way Home • Problem • Rather Be • See Through • Standing By.

00142426 P/V/G..$14.99

PENTATONIX – CHRISTMAS IS HERE!

Twelve piano/vocal/guitar arrangements of songs from Pentatonix's fourth holiday album, including: Greensleeves (Interlude) • Grown-Up Christmas List • Here Comes Santa Claus (Right Down Santa Claus Lane) • It's Beginning to Look a Lot like Christmas • Jingle Bells • Making Christmas • Rockin' Around the Christmas Tree • Sweater Weather • Waltz of the Flowers • What Christmas Means to Me • When You Believe • Where Are You Christmas?.

00288057 P/V/G..$17.99

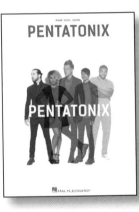

PENTATONIX

The 2015 album release by these a cappella masters and winners of NBC's *The Sing Off* topped the Billboard 200 album charts and features all original material. Our matching songbook features piano/vocal/guitar arrangements with the piano part covering all the vocal harmonies for all 16 songs from the CD, including: Can't Sleep Love • Cracked • If I Ever Fall in Love • Ref • Sing • Take Me Home • and more.

00155228 P/V/G..$19.99

PENTATONIX – PTX PRESENTS: TOP POP, VOL. 1

This sixth studio release from a cappella masters Pentatonix is their first to include new bass vocalist Matt Sallee. Our songbook features piano/vocal/guitar arrangements for all of the pop/R&B classic songs on the album: Attention • Finesse • New Rules x Are You That Somebody • Havana • Perfect • Feel It Still • Despacito x Shape of You • Issues • Praying • Sorry Not Sorry • Stay.

00278900 P/V/G..$17.99

PENTATONIX – THAT'S CHRISTMAS TO ME

This collection provides piano, vocal and guitar arrangements corresponding to the unique a cappella vocal treatments that Pentatonix presented on their holiday CD. Songs: Dance of the Sugar Plum Fairy • Winter Wonderland/Don't Worry, Be Happy • Hark! The Herald Angels Sing • Let It Go • Mary, Did You Know? • It's the Most Wonderful Time of the Year • Santa Claus Is Comin' to Town • Silent Night • Sleigh Ride • That's Christmas to Me • White Winter Hymnal.

00172460 P/V/G..$19.99

HAL•LEONARD®

www.halleonard.com

Prices, contents, and availability subject to change without notice.